ABOLITIONISTS JOIN THE FIGHT

D1004756

COMPILED BY JOANNE RANDOLPH
★

PowerKiDS
press.

Published in 2018 by The Rosen Publishing Group, Inc.
29 East 21st Street, New York, NY 10010

"Abolitionists Join the Struggle" by Heather Cox Richardson from Cobblestone Magazine (November 2016)
"Unlikely Election" by Michael Green from Cobblestone Magazine (November 2016)

Cataloging-in-Publication Data

Names: Randolph, Joanne.
Title: Abolitionists join the fight / compiled by Joanne Randolph.
Description: New York : PowerKids Press, 2018. | Series: The Civil War and Reconstruction: rebellion and rebuilding | Includes glossary and index.
Identifiers: LCCN ISBN 9781538340783 (pbk.) | ISBN 9781538340776 (library bound) | ISBN 9781538340790 (6 pack)
Subjects: LCSH: Abolitionists--United States--History--19th century--Juvenile literature. | Antislavery movements--United States--History--19th century--Juvenile literature. | Slaves--Emancipation--United States--Juvenile literature.
Classification: LCC E449.R44 A265 2018 | DDC 973.7'114--dc23

Designer: Katelyn E. Reynolds
Editor: Joanne Randolph

Photo credits: Cvr, p. 1 Stock Montage/Getty Images; cvr, pp. 1–32 (background texture) javarman/Shutterstock.com; cvr, pp. 1–32 (flags) cybrain/Shutterstock.com; cvr, pp. 1–32 (scroll) Seregam/Shutterstock.com; p. 5 The Print Collector/Getty Images; p. 6 Hulton Archive/Getty Images; pp. 7, 8 (all), 12, 15, 20, 21, 24, 25, 26, 28, 29 courtesy of the Library of Congress; p. 11 SuperStock/Getty Imsges; p. 13 © CORBIS/Corbis via Getty Images; pp. 14, 17 Bettmann/Getty Images; p. 19 Historica Graphica Collection/Heritage Images/Getty Images; p. 22 National Portrait Gallery, Washington/Accession number NPG.65.48/Wikipedia.org; p. 23 Yosihait/Wikipedia.org.

Manufactured in the United States of America

CPSIA Compliance Information: Batch #CS18PK: For Further Information contact Rosen Publishing, New York, New York at 1-800-237-9932.

CONTENTS

WORDS IN THE GLOSSARY APPEAR
IN **BOLD** TYPE THE FIRST TIME
THEY ARE USED IN THE TEXT.

★

PUTTING AN END TO SLAVERY

For some Americans, the issue of slavery hung on a single question: Should a nation that valued liberty hold people as slaves? Across the nation, **abolitionists**—people who wanted to end slavery and immediately **emancipate** all enslaved people—organized to stop it. Free black Americans in the North had worked hard to rescue **fugitive** slaves from slave catchers and to end slavery since at least the 1820s, but white Americans had paid them little attention. Slowly, though, the abolitionist movement grew among white Americans in the North, too.

By 1820, every state in the North had either prohibited slavery or provided for slavery's gradual abolition. Abolitionists made the **institution** of slavery and the evils of human **bondage** a **moral** and political issue. Southerners, meanwhile, resented what they saw as interference in their affairs. They believed that laws passed by Congress favored northern industry at the expense of southern agriculture.

THE SOUTH'S ECONOMY RELIED HEAVILY ON
AGRICULTURE, PARTICULARLY ON THE GROWTH OF
COTTON. HERE, SLAVES LABOR OVER HARVESTED
COTTON AS A WHITE MAN OVERSEES THEIR WORK.

★

5

WRITING ABOUT IT

On January 1, 1831, abolitionist William Lloyd Garrison published the first issue of a newspaper dedicated to ending slavery. In *The Liberator*, Garrison vowed that he would not stop until enslaved people were free. At the same time that abolitionists began organizing, slave owners became more **brutal** in their treatment and punishment of enslaved people who tried to fight for freedom.

That August, the slave rebellion in Virginia led by Nat Turner convinced most white southerners that freeing the slaves would be dangerous. They began to defend slavery and to insist that it be extended.

WILLIAM LLOYD GARRISON WAS BOTH AN ABOLITIONIST AND AN ANTI-UNIONIST. HE BELIEVED THAT THE CONSTITUTION WAS A PROSLAVERY DOCUMENT.

★

WOMEN ABOLITIONISTS, SUCH AS
THE GRIMKÉ SISTERS, LUCRETIA MOTT, AND
ELIZABETH CADY STANTON, LATER BECAME
LEADERS IN THE WOMEN'S SUFFRAGE MOVEMENT.

★

SARAH MOORE GRIMKÉ

ANGELINA EMILY GRIMKÉ

LUCRETIA MOTT

ELIZABETH CADY STANTON

In the 1830s, abolitionists organized antislavery societies and recruited women to participate in them. Two sisters, Sarah Moore Grimké and Angelina Emily Grimké, became important speakers for the cause. They had grown up in a wealthy slaveholding family in the South, and they had seen the cruelties and violence of slavery firsthand. They had moved to the North, where their spoken and written words against slavery **resonated** with listeners and readers.

Organizers mailed the Grimkés' writings, along with other abolitionist **literature**, through the U.S. mail system. When southern leaders complained that those books and pamphlets could cause a slave uprising, postmasters refused to deliver them. At the same time, abolitionists began to flood Congress with **petitions** to end slavery. Southerners forced through a "gag rule" in 1836, which said that Congress would immediately table, or lay aside, all those slavery-related petitions without considering them.

Most white northerners did not have strong opinions about slavery, but southern attacks on the U.S. mail and the constitutional right of Americans to petition the government changed things. Abolitionists warned that slave owners were trying to destroy freedom for everyone—white Americans as well as black slaves. They called the political influence of slave owners Slave Power. Abolitionists warned against the Slave Power taking control of the government.

THE STRUGGLE CONTINUES

In the 1840s, abolitionists continued to speak and write about the evils of slavery. On a lecture tour in 1841, former Maryland slave Frederick Douglass eloquently shared his story of abuse and slavery and his daring escape to the North and to freedom. Five years later, he began publishing *The North Star*, an antislavery newspaper that discussed abolition as part of an international movement for human freedom. Douglass helped black abolitionists to form their own organizations because white abolitionists, such as Garrison, did not always treat black Americans as equals.

Tension over slavery mounted as abolitionists constantly attacked the institution and southern slaveholders increasingly defended it. Rather than a necessary evil, southern whites began to say that slavery was part of God's plan. They held up their vast wealth as proof that their system must be blessed. They noted that slavery had been part of the nation when the Constitution was written.

They pointed out that many of the Founding Fathers, including George Washington and Thomas Jefferson, had held slaves. They argued that slavery was a "**benevolent** institution," and that slaves were happy and well cared for. Those arguments just made abolitionists more determined to end slavery.

FREDERICK DOUGLASS—ESCAPED SLAVE, LECTURER, NEWSPAPERMAN, AND AUTHOR—BECAME A POWERFUL VOICE IN THE ABOLITIONIST CAUSE.

A NATION DIVIDED

By 1850, the struggle over slavery could not be contained. In 1848, the nation had acquired a vast new territory that stretched all the way to the Pacific Ocean. The new territory was not covered by the Missouri Compromise, which divided the continent between slave states and free states. Both sides prepared for a battle. At the last minute, congressmen hammered out a compromise that included a strong fugitive slave law. The law required northerners to return escaped slaves to their masters.

CAUTION!!

COLORED PEOPLE

OF BOSTON, ONE & ALL,

You are hereby respectfully CAUTIONED and advised, to avoid conversing with the

Watchmen and Police Officers of Boston,

For since the recent ORDER OF THE MAYOR & ALDERMEN, they are empowered to act as

KIDNAPPERS

AND

Slave Catchers,

And they have already been actually employed in KIDNAPPING, CATCHING, AND KEEPING SLAVES. Therefore, if you value your LIBERTY, and the *Welfare of the Fugitives* among you, *Shun* them in every possible manner, as so many *HOUNDS* on the track of the most unfortunate of your race.

Keep a Sharp Look Out for KIDNAPPERS, and have TOP EYE open.

APRIL 24, 1851.

THIS HANDBILL, PRINTED IN 1851, WAS DISTRIBUTED THROUGHOUT BOSTON, MASSACHUSETTS, TO WARN OF THE CONSEQUENCES OF THE FUGITIVE SLAVE LAW.

★

HARRIET BEECHER STOWE'S
BEST-SELLING NOVEL, *UNCLE TOM'S CABIN*,
DESCRIBED THE EVILS OF SLAVERY AND RALLIED
BOTH ABOLITIONISTS AND NORTHERNERS.

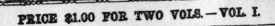

PRICE $1.00 FOR TWO VOLS.—VOL. I.

UNCLE TOM'S CABIN;

OR,

LIFE AMONG THE LOWLY.

BY

HARRIET BEECHER STOWE.

BOSTON:
PUBLISHED BY JOHN P. JEWETT & CO.
CLEVELAND, OHIO:
JEWETT, PROCTOR & WORTHINGTON.
1852.

Abolitionists were furious at the idea that they must act as slave catchers for slave owners. In 1852, abolitionist Harriet Beecher Stowe published a novel attacking the Fugitive Slave Act. *Uncle Tom's Cabin* became one of the best-selling novels of all time. It told the story of an elderly religious slave, Uncle Tom, and a young, light-skinned slave woman, Eliza. In the story, their master is in debt, so he sells Uncle Tom and young Harry, Eliza's son, because they are valuable slaves. The novel follows Uncle Tom as he is sold farther and farther south until he dies a martyr. Eliza escapes to save her son and carries him to freedom in Canada. The novel showed that there was no such thing as a benevolent form of slavery. It sold 300,000 copies in its first year, and plays based on it were performed across the North.

Northerners—not just abolitionists—were turning against slavery. When the events of the 1850s seemed to prove that the Slave Power was trying to take over the federal government, they were willing to fight to protect freedom. The abolitionists had helped lead the effort to change society.

HARRIET BEECHER STOWE

A WORLD VIEW

In the 18th century, an intellectual movement called the Enlightenment swept Europe and America. It emphasized rational thought and individualism. It encouraged leaders to create a world in which people could reach their highest potential. It supported the concept that people should not be stuck in the same positions for life just because of the circumstances under which they were born.

Those ideas of human freedom convinced many people that slavery must be abolished. In 1772, a famous legal case freeing a slave in Great Britain indicated that slavery would soon end there. In the years after the Revolutionary War (1775–1783), most northern states abolished slavery. In 1787, the Northwest Ordinance prohibited slavery in the Northwest Territory, which was the first organized territory in the new United States west of the original thirteen colonies.

Abolitionists in Great Britain and the United States called for the end of the Atlantic slave trade. Great Britain ended the importation of slaves in 1807. A year later, the United States also abolished the trade. Ending slavery where it already existed was harder. In 1833, Great Britain ended slavery in most of its empire, paying huge sums of money to compensate slave owners for the loss of their property. Ending slavery in the United States took 30 more years and a terrible civil war.

THIS 1854 MAP OF THE UNITED STATES SHOWS "AREAS OF SLAVERY AND FREEDOM" AS THEY STOOD BEFORE THE CIVIL WAR.

AN UNLIKELY ELECTION AND CIVIL WAR

Emotions were running high over the issue of slavery and whether the federal government had any right to regulate the practice in individual states. The abolitionists fanned the flames with their impassioned writing and speeches. The South clung desperately to what they saw as their only possible way of life. But what made them finally decide to **secede**?

When seven southern states seceded from the Union over the winter of 1860–61, they did so mainly as a result of the election of Abraham Lincoln as president. Lincoln was an unlikely winner from an unlikely party in an unlikely year.

LINCOLN OFTEN SPOKE OUT
AGAINST THE EXPANSION OF SLAVERY,
WHICH TURNED THE SLAVEHOLDING
SOUTHERN STATES AGAINST HIM.

19

MILLARD FILLMORE, SHOWN HERE, SERVED AS THE NATION'S THIRTEENTH PRESIDENT FROM 1850 TO 1853.

The unlikely party was the Republican party. It had emerged when the Democratic party split and the Whig party collapsed—both over the issue of slavery and its expansion into western territories. The Republicans mostly were antislavery northerners, and they had sought to win the presidency for the first time in 1856. In that year, they chose onetime explorer John C. Fremont as their candidate, and their party platform opposed the spread of slavery into new territories. That same year, another new political party— the American, or Know-Nothing, party— nominated former president Millard Fillmore. Their platform focused on stopping immigration.

JOHN C. FREMONT

James Buchanan served as president from 1857 to 1861. His failure to address the issue of slavery brought the nation to the very brink of Civil War.

The Democrats, meanwhile, were proslavery southerners or northerners who did not care whether or not slavery expanded into new western territory. The Democrats' nominee in 1856, Pennsylvanian James Buchanan, was a northerner. Since southerners refused to support any antislavery candidate, the election divided along regional lines. Buchanan ran against Fremont in the North and against Fillmore in the South. Buchanan won the 1856 election, but Fremont's showing gave the Republicans confidence. With the right candidate, they believed they could win in 1860.

1856 Democratic Poster

FREE TERRITORY FOR A FREE PEOPLE.

A. LINCOLN.

H. HAMLIN.

Initially the strongest candidate in the unlikely year of 1860 was Senator William H. Seward of New York. But he struck fellow Republicans as too radically antislavery to be elected. Critics accused him and his ally, New York political boss Thurlow Weed, of corruption. Powerful *New York Tribune* editor Horace Greeley had a personal grudge against Seward, and he used his influence to weaken Seward's candidacy.

Four other prominent men also sought the Republican nomination that year: Edward Bates of Missouri, U.S. senator Simon Cameron of Pennsylvania, Ohio governor Salmon P. Chase, and Abraham Lincoln of Illinois. While Seward was the front-runner, he needed more delegates than he had to win a majority and the nomination. Through the hard work of his supporters and allies, Lincoln somehow managed to come out on top and win his party's nomination.

WILLIAM H. SEWARD

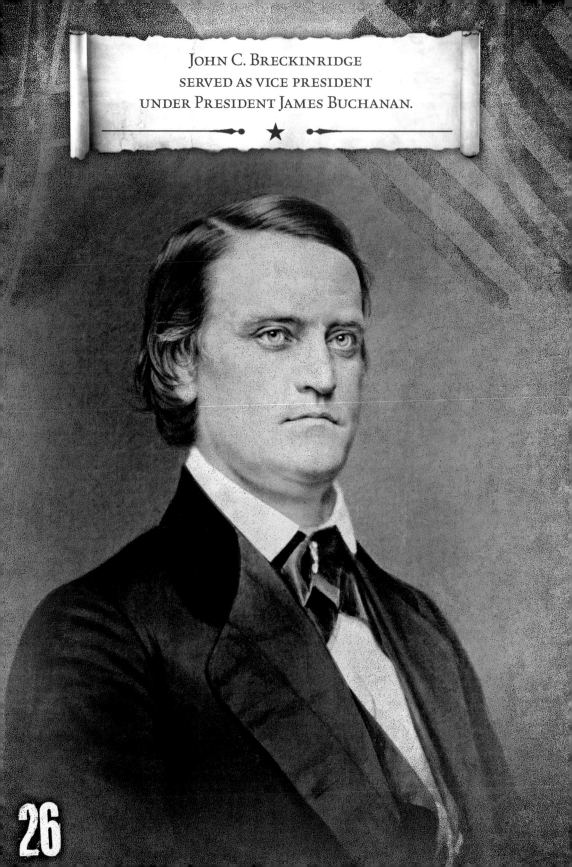

JOHN C. BRECKINRIDGE
SERVED AS VICE PRESIDENT
UNDER PRESIDENT JAMES BUCHANAN.

Democrats, meanwhile, had opened their convention in April in Charleston, South Carolina. Unable to agree on a nominee, they split into two meetings. In June, Northern Democrats met at a separate convention in Baltimore. They chose for president Senator Stephen A. Douglas of Illinois, who believed in popular sovereignty—that the people should vote on whether or not to expand slavery. Southern Democrats picked Vice President John C. Breckinridge of Kentucky, who stood by the *Dred Scott v. Sandford* U.S. Supreme Court decision, which said slavery could exist in any U.S. territories. Former Whigs and Know-Nothings, whose parties had collapsed, formed the Constitutional Union party. They took no position on slavery except to support the Constitution. That party nominated former Senator John Bell of Tennessee.

With the regions so divided, the election pitted Lincoln against Douglas in the North and Breckinridge against Bell in the South. Winning 180 electoral votes, Lincoln carried every northern state except Kentucky and New Jersey. Douglas won 12 electoral votes. Splitting the South, Breckinridge won 72 electoral votes and Bell came away with 39. Lincoln won only about 40 percent of the popular vote but an easy Electoral College majority.

THIS PHOTOGRAPH SHOWS
THE INAUGURATION OF PRESIDENT
ABRAHAM LINCOLN ON MARCH 4, 1861.

On the night of November 6, 1860, Lincoln learned the news and said, "God help me." He then went home and told his wife, "Mary, Mary, we are elected." The divisions within and between other parties contributed to his win.

Southerners had said they would leave the Union if a Republican won the White House. They had made that threat before. This time, in the unlikely election year of 1860, with all the heated discussions between abolitionists and those who wanted to keep slavery and the Southern way of life, they followed through. A month after Lincoln won the election, the first southern state, South Carolina, voted to secede. By April 1861, the nation was fighting a civil war.

THE FIRST FLAG OF INDEPENDENCE RAISED IN THE SOUTH

GLOSSARY

abolitionists: People who want to do away with slavery.

benevolent: Well-meaning and kindly; having a charitable purpose, rather than for profit.

bondage: The state of being a slave.

brutal: Savagely violent.

emancipate: Free someone from slavery or other legal, social, or political restrictions.

fugitive: A person who has escaped from a place and goes into hiding to avoid being recaptured.

institution: An established law, practice, or custom.

literature: Written works, especially those that are considered to be higher quality.

moral: Having to do with understanding the difference between right and wrong behavior.

petitions: Formal written request that has been signed by many people in order to appeal to an authority for a particular belief or cause.

resonated: Affected or appealed to someone in a personal or emotional way.

secede: Withdraw formally from membership in a federal union, an alliance, or a political or religious organization.

FOR MORE INFORMATION

★

BOOKS

Freedmen, Russel. *Abraham Lincoln and Frederick Douglass: The Story Behind an American Friendship.* New York: HMH Books for Young Readers, 2016.

Rau, Dana Meachen. *Who Was Harriet Beecher Stowe?* New York: Penguin Workshops, 2016.

WEBSITES

Abolitionist Movement
http://www.history.com/topics/black-history/abolitionist-movement

"I Will Be Heard!": Abolitionism in America
http://rmc.library.cornell.edu/abolitionism/abolitionists.htm

INDEX